AND NOW
A WORD
FROM OUR
MAKER

Lillenas Drama

AND NOW A WORD FROM OUR MAKER

Channel-Surf Your Way Through 28 Sketches and Monologues Based on Biblical Principles

by Martha Bolton

Author of *Let My People Laugh;*
Home, Home on the Stage;
A Funny Thing Happened to Me on
My Way Through the Bible, and so much more

illenas PUBLISHING COMPANY

KANSAS CITY, MO 64141

To Kiana . . .
May your life be full of joy,
love,
and may you always remember your Maker.

Contents

Acknowledgments 9

A Note from the Author 11

All's Forgiven on the Western Front 13

Come to Hakim's: A Commercial 16

True Stories of the Prison Patrol 17

Lost at Sea 19

Talkin' Hope 21

How's the Weather Up There? 24

No Greater Love Connection 25

You Can Bank on It: A Commercial 27

What a Dish! 28

All My Verses 29

Taking Stock 31

The Real Story 32

Donkey Talk: A Commercial 36

Emergency Rapture System 38

Wide World of Slingshots 39

Carpenter's Corner 41

Revelation Hot Line 43

. . . Got Hope?: A Commercial 44

What's Cookin'? 46

"Lost at Sea" Update 48

Sadducee TV 49

Evening at the Desert Improv 51

. . . Got Peace?: A Commercial 53

Sowin' Seeds 54

Eternity Awards Show 56

Solomon's Court TV 57

On the Road Again 59

. . . Got Love?: A Commercial 60

This Was Your Life 61

Acknowledgments

THANK YOU . . .

To my family, for not filing a class action suit for lung damage from prolonged exposure to dinner clouds.

To my sister, Melva, for her love, her servant's heart, and for buying me my first writer's magazine.

To my friend, Linda, my personal trainer and encourager. (Her goal is to get me under the hour mile.)

To my editor, Paul Miller, whose patience with deadlines I've often taxed but whose friendship is one of my most cherished. (One of these days I've just *got* to cook him a dinner!)

And to everyone at Lillenas Publishing and to the drama groups across the country and abroad, may God bless you as you continue to promote the Christian arts!

A Note from the Author

. . . *And Now a Word from Our Maker* is a collection of sketches and mono-logues that put biblical stories and principles into a television program setting. These can be performed individually or as a full evening's entertainment and ministry.

If the book is performed as a whole, I'd suggest using a sound effect of static during the blackouts between the sketches. The static should last only a few seconds but would give the feel of channel-surfing through the various stations.

You may also want to design the set to look like a giant television screen, complete with dials, and so forth. Your promotion handouts, programs, and tickets could resemble remote controls. If the program is staged in an area oth-er than the sanctuary, you might wish to serve popcorn and beverages.

Using just about every area of television—soap operas, westerns, talk shows, comedy shows, breaking news, commercials, and more—these scripts call for minimal props and small casts. They present spiritual truths in a unique and entertaining way, and since several of the sketches challenge the audience to evaluate their relationship to God, an invitation at the close of the program would be appropriate.

However your drama department uses these sketches, I pray they'll touch hearts and bring people to know the Lord.

And now a word from our Maker . . .

All's Forgiven on the Western Front

Characters:
> Drill Sergeant
> Private Cunningham
> General
> Narrator
> Four or five Soldiers (nonspeaking roles)

Setting: Army camp

Props: Bible (in the General's uniform pocket)

Costumes: Military uniforms, according to rank. Private Cunningham's head and leg are bandaged, and he's leaning on a crutch. His uniform is in a state of disarray.

(*Sketch opens with a freeze-frame of the* Soldiers *standing center stage.* Private Cunningham *is weak and barely able to hold himself up.* Sergeant *is standing nearby.* Narrator *is at the side of the stage.*)

Narrator: And now we return to our movie of the week, *All's Forgiven on the Western Front.*

(Narrator *exits. The characters now come alive.*)

Sergeant (*firmly, as he paces in front of soldiers*): Ten-hut! (Cunningham *tries to stand at attention, but can barely do it.*) Ten-hut! (Cunningham *makes another attempt, but is too weak.* Sergeant *stops in front of him.*) Look at yourself, soldier. You're a disgrace to your uniform!

Cunningham (*weakly*): I just returned from battle.

Sergeant: I caaan't heeear you!

Cunningham: I just returned from battle, *sir!*

Sergeant (*inspecting* Cunningham's *uniform*): Is that blood?

Cunningham: I took a hit, sir.

Sergeant: You've fallen in the line of duty?

Cunningham: I'll be all right. I just need a little help standing right now.

Sergeant: Help standing? What do you want us to do, carry you around on a fluffy little pillow?

Cunningham: No, sir. I just . . .

13

SERGEANT (*cutting in*): A wounded soldier is a soldier who has failed. I don't tolerate failure, son.

CUNNINGHAM: I've been in the battle a long time, sir. This is the first time I've fallen.

SERGEANT: One time, one hundred times. A wounded soldier has no place in a perfect army! (GENERAL *enters.* SERGEANT *salutes him, then turns to* CUNNINGHAM.) Ten-hut! (CUNNINGHAM *tries to salute* GENERAL, *but he's too weak.*) Ten-hut! (CUNNINGHAM *tries again, but can't.*)

GENERAL: Is there a problem, Sergeant?

SERGEANT: This soldier has just returned from battle, sir. I apologize for his appearance.

GENERAL (*to* CUNNINGHAM): Front line?

CUNNINGHAM: Yes, I . . .

SERGEANT (*cutting in*): He took a hit. But don't worry. The firing squad will take care of him at daybreak.

GENERAL: Firing squad?

CUNNINGHAM: . . . Firing squad?

GENERAL: What kind of an army shoots its own wounded, Sergeant?

SERGEANT: A *perfect* one, sir. In this army, there's zero tolerance for failure.

GENERAL: And whose rule is *that?*

SERGEANT: My own rule, sir. Soldiers like this bring shame to us all.

GENERAL: And just how many *perfect* soldiers do you have under your command?

SERGEANT: Well . . . (*Thinks a moment*) None, sir. They all failed, the losers. But they're gone now. And this one will be gone soon too.

GENERAL: Isn't that *my* decision to make?

SERGEANT: I know how busy you are, sir. I just thought I'd offer my assistance. You know, weed out the weaker ones.

GENERAL: Apparently, Sergeant, you've misread your manual. Your goal is to build up the weaker ones, not weed them out.

SERGEANT: But, General, I'm not asking anything of my troops that I don't demand of myself. My uniform's pressed, my gig line's straight. You won't find a single thing on me that's out of line.

GENERAL: . . . Except your heart. (*A beat*) When's the last time you were on the front line, Sergeant?

SERGEANT: Well, I . . . uh . . .

GENERAL: Your compassion's getting a little rusty. Maybe it's time you saw a little front line action.

SERGEANT: Uh . . . perhaps I *was* a little too hard on him.

GENERAL: Sergeant, as the highest-ranking officer in this army, I'm granting this soldier a second chance.

CUNNINGHAM: A second chance, sir?

GENERAL: That's right, soldier. And a third and a fourth if need be. Perfection is the goal of this army, not a minimum requirement. And we *do* take care of our wounded.

CUNNINGHAM: Thank you, sir.

SERGEANT: So you're saying if a soldier falls in battle, we stop and help him back up.

GENERAL *(taking Bible from his pocket):* It's in the manual.

SERGEANT: But, General, I was always taught that there's *no excuse* for failure.

GENERAL: I don't know who your training officer was, Sergeant, but in *this* army, the only thing there's no excuse for is unforgiveness. *(Straightens* CUNNINGHAM's *uniform)* And don't worry, soldier, you just take this *(hands him the Bible),* read it every day, and when you're feeling strong enough again, get back into the battle.

CUNNINGHAM: I will, General. *(Salutes him)* You can count on me.

GENERAL: I know I can, son. Now, c'mon . . . *(Puts his arms on shoulders of* SERGEANT *and* CUNNINGHAM *and as they start to exit . . .)* We've got a war to win!

SERGEANT: But what about me?

(GENERAL *stops and turns back toward* SERGEANT.)

GENERAL: We want you back in the battle, too, only this time, remember who the enemy is. (GENERAL *and* CUNNINGHAM *exit.)*

(Blackout)

Come to Hakim's

A Commercial

Character: HAKIM

Setting: Hakim's Pre-Owned Chariots dealership

Props: A chariot or reasonable facsimile

       (Can be as simple or elaborate as your budget will allow. It's a used chariot, so it doesn't have to look that great.)

    Four signs: One that says "300 shekels"

        One that says "200 shekels"

        One that says "150 shekels"

        One that says "100 shekels"

Costumes: Bible era clothing

(Sketch opens with HAKIM *standing in front of a chariot. There is a sign on the chariot that says "300 shekels." The other signs are behind them.)*

(Quickly and as if into camera) Folks! You want chariots? I've got chariots! Luxury models, compact models, sports models, two horsepower, four horsepower, yes, even *six* horsepower chariots! Frieeeennnnnds, I've got 'em all, so come on down to *Hakim's Pre-Owned Chariots* where we're right in the middle of our annual Moonlight Madness Sale!

But I can't afford a chariot, you say? Not true at Hakim's! *(Walks over to chariot)* Take a look at this baby. This 1957 B.C. convertible offers plenty of legroom and natural air conditioning. And it's barely broken in, folks! Just 10,000 miles on it! That's right. 10,000 miles! . . . It was owned by a little old lady who only drove it to the Sunday morning chariot races.

So, how much do you think a beauty like this would go for . . . 300 shekels? No! *(Tosses sign away, revealing the "200 shekels" sign underneath)* 200 shekels? No! *(Tosses the sign away, revealing "150 shekels" sign)* Not even 150 shekels! Folks, this chariot can be yours for only . . . *(Tosses "150 shekels" sign away, revealing "100 shekels" sign)* 100 shekels! Yes, you heard me right, folks. 100 shekels! *Someone better put me away! I've gone completely mad!* 100 shekels! That's below my cost! But then, you know my motto. "I'm not here to make money. *(Places hand over heart and smiles innocently)* I just want to *help* my fellowman!"

So, come on down and take this baby out for a test run. Or any one of my pre-owned chariots. I guarantee there's one here you'll like. And don't forget—we take trade-ins and offer 48 percent financing . . . on approved credit.

. . . That's Hakim's Pre-Owned Chariots, where the highway meets the byway. Swing on by and drive one of our chariots home today! *(A beat)* . . . Tow service not included.

(Blackout)

True Stories of the Prison Patrol

Characters:
> HOST
> GUARD

Setting: Prison

Props: Handheld microphone

Costumes: Modern-day wear for HOST
> Bible era guard wear for GUARD

(Sketch opens with the GUARD, center stage. HOST approaches.)

HOST *(to audience):* Today on "True Stories of the Prison Patrol," we'll hear the incredible tale of the prison guard who was assigned to the cell of Paul and Silas. *(Walks over to GUARD)* Excuse me, officer . . .

GUARD: Yes?

HOST: I'm from "True Stories of the Prison Patrol." I'd like to talk with you about two prisoners who were assigned to you?

GUARD: Do you have their booking number?

HOST: No. But their names are Paul and Silas.

GUARD: Now there's two prisoners I'll *never* forget!

HOST: Why's that?

GUARD: Well, most prisoners get in fights with the other inmates, yell at the guards, or start a riot. Paul and Silas were the only two who ever sat around singing praise songs.

HOST: They sang *praise songs* in prison?

GUARD: Wore out three hymnals. They'd sing every single verse of every single song. Over and over and over again. I've never seen anything like it. Here were two guys whose freedom had been taken from them, and for what? For stealing? For killing? No. For preaching the gospel of Jesus Christ.

HOST: They didn't appeal?

GUARD: They were thrown in this cold, dirty prison, their feet were in stocks, and all they can do is sing 'bout how good their God is.

HOST: Real optimists, huh?

GUARD: Optimists? They didn't see the glass as half-full. They saw the *well behind it!*

HOST: So, what'd you do?

GUARD: Listened. What else could I do? I was a captive audience, you know. Had my own personal concert every night.

HOST: That's better than a riot, I guess.

GUARD: One night, we even had *special effects.*

HOST: Special effects?

GUARD: It was a night I'll never forget. Paul and Silas were on the second chorus of their third song, and all of a sudden I hear this rumbling noise. The earth starts shaking, things are falling all around us.

HOST: An earthquake?

GUARD: I figure it's a 6-, 7-, maybe even an 8-pointer. I don't know . . . we didn't have our seismograph hooked up that night. Felt like the epicenter was right under our jail cell.

HOST: What'd the prisoners do?

GUARD: That's the amazing thing. The bands on all the prisoners fell off and their stocks opened. After the shaking stopped, I don't see Paul and Silas anywhere. I figure my life's over. The magistrates don't look too kindly on guards who misplace their prisoners. But then I hear Paul's voice telling me not to panic, that all the prisoners are *still there.*

HOST: They didn't even try to escape?

GUARD (*shakes head*): I knew right then and there that what they had inside them, what they were singing about, was *real.* The next thing I know I'm asking them what I need to do to be saved.

HOST: You became a believer?

GUARD: I became a believer, my family became believers, and who knows how many other prisoners were affected by the testimony of these two men. And after the earthquake, the magistrates even decided to give them their freedom.

HOST: That's quite a story!

GUARD: Yeah . . . it just goes to show you, you never know what can happen when you choose to live in praise instead of pity.

(Blackout)

Lost at Sea

Characters:
    ANNOUNCER
    NEWS REPORTER
    EYEWITNESS
Setting: The seaside
Props: Handheld microphone
Costume: Bible era wear

ANNOUNCER *(over P.A.):* We interrupt this program to bring you the following special news bulletin . . .

(Lights come up and we see REPORTER *on the sea shore, holding the microphone in his hand.* EYEWITNESS *is standing near him.)*

REPORTER: So far there's been no sign of the man who was lost at sea late last night. Identified only as Jonah, apparently he was en route to the city of Tarshish when the unfortunate incident occurred. We have with us right now an eyewitness to the tragedy. *(Moves toward* EYEWITNESS*)* Sir, can you tell us exactly what happened last night?

EYEWITNESS *(nervously, as if hiding something):* I was on the boat and a man went overboard. That's all I know. Now if you'll excuse me . . .

REPORTER: The waters were pretty rough last night.

EYEWITNESS: We hit a bad storm, yes . . . I really have to be going now.

REPORTER: So, is that how Jonah fell overboard? The storm?

EYEWITNESS: Uh . . . yes . . . I guess so.

REPORTER: He *did* fall overboard, didn't he?

EYEWITNESS: Look, I had nothing to do with it. It was the others . . .

REPORTER: Nothing to do with what, sir?

EYEWITNESS: Nothing. *(He starts to walk off, then stops and turns back.)* OK . . . I'll tell you the truth. He didn't exactly *fall* overboard.

REPORTER: Are you suggesting *foul play?*

EYEWITNESS: We only did what he asked us to do.

REPORTER: Jonah asked all of you to throw him into the raging sea where he'd surely drown?

EYEWITNESS: Yes.

REPORTER: And you did it?

EYEWITNESS: Look, he said the storm was on account of his disobedience to . . . well, to God, and if we threw him overboard, the sea would calm.

REPORTER: So you figured it was worth a shot?

EYEWITNESS: We were desperate. The boat was ready to capsize. We would have tried anything.

REPORTER: Then what happened?

EYEWITNESS: It was amazing. Once Jonah was out of the boat, the sea barely had a ripple.

REPORTER: Where's Jonah now?

EYEWITNESS *(shakes head):* One of the other passengers said he saw a big fish, probably a whale, circling him, and . . . well, I don't even want to think about it.

REPORTER: That's all right, sir. But we do thank you for speaking with us today. I know it's been painful. (EYEWITNESS *nods, obviously shaken, then walks off.* REPORTER *turns to audience, as if speaking into the camera.)* This has been a Tarshish News Breaking Story. We now return to our regularly scheduled programming . . .

(Blackout)

Talkin' Hope

Characters:
> RICHARD CHAMBERS: *host*
> JOSHUA
> SHAPHAT
> PRODUCER

Setting: "The Negative Side" talk show

Props: Handheld microphone
> Two chairs
> Book, titled *Giant Co-Dependents and Those Who Love Them*

Costumes: Modern-day wear for RICHARD
> Bible era clothing for JOSHUA and SHAPHAT

(Sketch opens with JOSHUA and SHAPHAT seated center stage. SHAPHAT has the book in his hand. RICHARD, standing with microphone in hand, addresses the audience.)

RICHARD: I'm Richard Chambers, and thanks for tuning in to "The Negative Side" talk show. Today our topic is "Giants—Of Course, We Should Fear Them." As you know, this is a follow-up to last week's shows, "Giant Makeovers," and "Mothers of Giants Who've Seen Elvis." Our guests are 2 of the 10 spies who went into the Promised Land to see if it was everything the Lord said it would be. *(To JOSHUA and SHAPHAT)* Thank you, gentlemen, for joining us today. *(JOSHUA and SHAPHAT nod a greeting.)* We'll begin with Joshua . . . Sir, could you tell us in your own words exactly what you saw when you and the others entered the Promised Land?

SHAPHAT *(cutting in):* Giants! We saw giants! Hundreds of them! Thousands of them! Hundreds of thou . . . *(JOSHUA gives SHAPHAT a look. SHAPHAT tapers off midsentence.)*

RICHARD *(to JOSHUA):* So, you *did* see giants?

JOSHUA: Sure, there were giants, but they're only a *small* part of the story.

SHAPHAT: *Small* part? The only part of this story that was small was *us!*

RICHARD: Just how big were these giants?

SHAPHAT: We looked like grasshoppers next to them!

RICHARD *(to JOSHUA):* Is that true?

JOSHUA: Compared to *us*, they were giants. Compared to *God*, they were wimps. Now, getting back to the Promised Land . . .

SHAPHAT: They'd rather hear about the giants.

JOSHUA: No, they wouldn't. They don't want to dwell on the negative.

RICHARD: Well, actually, Joshua, we would. We are a talk show, you know. It's how we get ratings.

JOSHUA: But the Promised Land was flowing with milk and honey. And the bunches of grapes there were so big, it took *two* men to carry them. We didn't even *try* to lift their watermelons!

RICHARD *(yawning):* That's nice. *(A beat)* Now, about those giants . . .

SHAPHAT: Would this be a good time to mention my book? *(He shows his book to the "camera.")*

JOSHUA *(to RICHARD, continuing):* Well, I'd prefer to see possibilities rather than hopelessness. I'd rather look beyond the giants and see the greatness of God.

RICHARD: Yes, well . . . I think it's time for a commercial break. *(Gives the cut sign, presumably to a director offstage.)*

JOSHUA: Don't you want to hear what I have to say?

RICHARD: Not really. This is sweeps week.

JOSHUA: Give the people something to hope for, something to believe in, and just watch your ratings soar . . .

RICHARD *(calling offstage while giving the "cut" sign again):* Commercial . . . commercial . . .

JOSHUA *(grabs the microphone):* You can try to cut me off. *(As if into camera)* You at home can turn the channel. But my message will still get through somehow. A message of hope not fear. A challenge for you to look at the promised land in your life, not the giants.

RICHARD: . . . Where do we get these guests? *(Grabs the microphone back)*

SHAPHAT *(to RICHARD):* Can I plug my book now? The title is *(holds up book again.)* Co-Dependent Giants and Those Who Love Them.

JOSHUA *(to RICHARD):* Forget his book. Let me tell you more about the Promised Land . . . *(As JOSHUA ad-libs a description of the Promised Land, i.e., "It's beautiful," "I've never seen such green grass, such clear rivers," etc.)*

RICHARD: There goes my career! My ratings are plummeting! The show's going to get canceled! It's . . . (PRODUCER *enters and whispers something to* RICHARD.) No kidding? (PRODUCER *exits.* RICHARD *turns to* JOSHUA.)

SHAPHAT: Does he want me to give the 800 number for my book?

RICHARD: My producer just told me my ratings are going through the roof! I guess a positive attitude really *does* pay off.

JOSHUA: Positively!

RICHARD: So, Joshua, can you come back tomorrow and tell us more about this Promised Land?

JOSHUA: There's nothing I'd like better.

RICHARD *(to audience, as if into camera)*: And that's going to do it for this episode of "The Negative Side" talk show. Don't forget to tune in tomorrow for more good news from Joshua.

(Blackout. No television static after this blackout. After a few seconds, the lights come back up. RICHARD and JOSHUA have left the stage. Only SHAPHAT remains seated. He's holding up his book again.)

SHAPHAT: . . . Did I mention it's only $8.95?

(Blackout)

How's the Weather Up There?

Character:
> METEOROLOGIST (may be played by male or female)

Setting: The Eternity Weather Channel

Props: Several weather maps, including a heaven's weather map and a hell's weather map

> Sign that says "Eternity Weather Channel"

Costume: Modern-day wear

(Sketch opens with our METEOROLOGIST *standing in front of the weather maps, facing the audience.)*

This is the Eternity Weather Channel with tonight's Eternity Weather report. From our satellite readings, it doesn't look like we'll be having much of a change in our weather patterns any time soon.

(Walks over to heaven's weather map) Heaven continues to enjoy mild temperatures and beautifully clear skies. No wonder they call it Paradise, folks. It's absolutely gorgeous! The waters are steady and calm on the Crystal Sea, and there's a slight breeze from the flap of low flying angels' wings. If you're headed to this region, I'd have to say you've made an excellent destination choice.

Meanwhile, directly south of there *(turns to hell's weather map)* they're having a record-breaking heat wave with no end in sight. Temperatures in the Lake of Fire and surrounding areas continue to soar. 1,000 . . . 2,000 degrees. It's a scorcher, folks. There's not a sunscreen on the market strong enough for that kind of heat. We're hundreds of miles away, and it's already melted our weather equipment and most of my dental work. If your eternity travel plans take you anywhere near this area, I'd strongly advise making a change immediately. Turn around and set your sights north . . . *way north.*

This is the Eternity Weather Channel, giving you continuous weather updates to help you decide where *you* want to spend eternity!

(Blackout)

No Greater Love Connection

Characters:
> ANNOUNCER (over P.A.)
> CHUCK NEWLY
> RANDY ACKERMAN

Setting: The "No Greater Love Connection" set

Props: Two chairs
> Sign that says "No Greater Love Connection"

Costumes: Modern-day wear

(Sketch opens with CHUCK *standing center stage)*

ANNOUNCER *(over P.A.):* And now, let's hear it for the host of our show, Chuck Newly . . .

*(*CHUCK *enters and stands center stage.)*

CHUCK: Thank you, and welcome to "No Greater Love Connection." . . . And now, let's meet our first contestant . . . He was lost; he was lonely; he was at the end of his rope. He's back today to tell us all about his No Greater Love Connection. Ladies and gentlemen, let's give a warm welcome to . . . Randy Ackerman . . . (RANDY *enters. They shake hands and both take a seat.)* Randy, tell us a little something about yourself.

RANDY: Well, Chuck, I was feeling pretty down. There was an emptiness inside of me. I didn't have a direction, a purpose.

CHUCK: That's why you came to us.

RANDY: Exactly.

CHUCK: . . . So, where were you born, Randy?

RANDY: I was born into sin, Chuck.

CHUCK: Weren't we *all.*

RANDY: Yes, but the person I met through the "No Greater Love Connection" died for those sins some 2,000 years ago.

CHUCK: He paid the price?

RANDY: Wiped my slate completely clean.

CHUCK: So it sounds like the two of you really hit it off.

RANDY: He knew everything about me, but loved me anyway.

CHUCK: And that's just what you were looking for?

RANDY: Better. I can talk to Him any time of the day or night.

CHUCK: You've got his beeper number?

RANDY: He doesn't have a beeper, but I can reach Him 24-7. He's ready to listen whenever I'm feeling down or just need to talk. In fact, He knows what I need before I even ask Him.

CHUCK: So, in other words, you made a No Greater Love Connection.

RANDY: I sure did. The emptiness inside me is filled now, and I just want to live the rest of my life for Him.

CHUCK: Then, you're wanting to continue this relationship?

RANDY: Absolutely. The man gave His life for me on the Cross, Chuck. How can I refuse a love like that?

CHUCK: Unfortunately, Randy, a lot of people do.

(Blackout)

You Can Bank On It

Character:
    ACCOUNTANT

Setting: The Let Not Your Heart Be Troubled Financial Institution

Props: Freestanding counter
    Sign that says "Let Not Your Heart Be Troubled Financial Institution"

Costume: Modern-day wear

(Monologue opens with ACCOUNTATNT *standing behind counter. The sign is either on the counter or on a wall behind him.)*

Do you have trouble sleeping because you're worried what tomorrow will bring? Do you wonder if your ship is *ever* going to come in, or are they going to have to drag the bottom of the ocean for it? If this sounds like you, then call us today at the Let Not Your Heart Be Troubled Financial Institution. We're not a bank, lender, or credit card company. We don't pay interest, charge interest, or give away any toasters. We just remind you that you're a child of the King and in all our years in business we've "never seen the righteous forsaken or His seed out begging for bread." . . . So, don't let worry steal your joy. Follow scriptural principles with your finances, and put God first in both your life and your wallet. After all, when's the last time you saw a sparrow carrying a tin cup in his wing or the lilies of the field holding a sign that says, "Will bloom for food?" . . . C'mon . . . give us a call today at 1-800-He-Cares. That's 1-800-He-Cares, and leave your troubles with Him.

(Blackout)

What a Dish!

Character:
> JULIA WILD

Setting: The "'What a Dish!' Cooking Show"

Props: Pots
> Pans
> Spoon
> Freestanding kitchen counter
> 3 dozen locusts (if not available at your neighborhood grocery store, use rubber grasshoppers)
> Sign above or on the counter that says "'What a Dish!' Cooking Show"

Costumes: Bible era clothing

(Sketch opens with JULIA *standing center stage behind the counter. Pots and pans are on the counter. She's stirring one pot.)*

(In a high-pitched voice) Today, we're going to be making one of John the Baptist's favorite dishes—locusts and honey.

This snack is low in fat, high in protein, and quick and easy to prepare. It's perfect for those times when you just want to get out and be alone in the wilderness. First, you're going to need about three dozen locusts. Make sure they're fresh, never frozen. *(Using a string unseen by the audience, have one of the "locusts" appear to jump up out of the pot. She knocks it back in.)* Get back in there! . . . Frisky little creatures, aren't they?

Now then, once they're in your pan, add two tablespoons of oil, salt and pepper to taste, then cover ever so . . . *(another one tries to jump out just as she slams down the lid on the pot)* quickly! Now, slowly cook the locust over medium heat for about 10 minutes. Locusts will be tender and flaky, and taste something like chicken. I recommend that you serve them hot with plenty of honey for dipping.

Company coming? Try serving "locust kabobs" or my crowd-pleasing favorite "locust hot wings."

Locusts—the white meat you've probably never even thought about.

Until next time, this is Julia Wild saying, "Bon appétit."

(Blackout)

All My Verses

Characters:
> ANNOUNCER
> MARLENE WILLIAMS

Setting: Living room

Props: Accent table
> Chair
> Bible verse holder, filled with Bible verses written on little ticket-sized
>> cards
> Telephone
> Bible

Costumes: Modern-day wear

Sound Effects:
> Soap opera organ music, optional
> Telephone ring
> Doorbell ring

(Sketch opens with MARLENE *pacing. The Bible verse holder and Bible verses are on the coffee table, as well as the Bible. As the* ANNOUNCER *speaks,* MARLENE *reacts accordingly.)*

ANNOUNCER *(over P.A.):* When we last left Marlene Williams, she was about to decide how much of God's Word she was going to follow and how much of it she would ignore. Would she obey all Ten Commandments or pretend every other one was a misprint? Would she *have* an attitude over the Beatitudes? Would she trust in all of God's promises or just the ones that don't require much faith? And finally, would she wonder how she's hearing me over her P.A. system when she doesn't even have a P.A. system? *(*MARLENE *looks around as if trying to figure out where the voice is coming from.)* The answers to these and other probing questions will be answered today on the one millionth, four hundred and fifty thousandth episode of . . . *All My Verses.*

*(*MARLENE *stops pacing and looks at the Bible verse holder.)*

MARLENE: All right . . . just *one* more time. I'm gonna pick one of these Bible verses and *this* time, it'd better be one I can follow. *(She draws one, then reads.)* "A gossip betrays a confidence, but a trustworthy man keeps a secret."

> Well, struck out again. I can't follow a verse like *that. (She puts the verse back in the holder.)* . . . At least, not until I've told everyone on my phone chain that juicy half-truth I heard today about Ralph Wilson . . . Guess I'll just have to pick another verse for today. *(She draws a verse and starts to read. SFX: phone rings. Into phone . . .)* Hello? . . . This is *who?* . . .

First Bank MasterCard? And who did you say you wanted? . . . Marlene Williams? *(Disguising her voice)* Sorry, she no live here. You dial wrong number. *(Hangs up)* Bill collectors! Boy, I sure hope this is a verse I can use. *(Reads from card)* "Bread of deceit is sweet to a man: but afterwards his mouth shall be filled with gravel." *(She mimes as if she's got a mouthful of gravel, then puts that card back too.)*

C'mon, where are the genealogies? They're usually safe. *(Starts to draw another verse)* All I'm asking for is one or two "begats." That's all. *(SFX: doorbell rings. She walks to the side of the stage and mimes opening the door.)*

Yes, I'm the lady of the house . . . You're collecting for a charity? . . . *(Perturbed)* I was trying to find a scripture for today, and you interrupted me to *ask for money?* If I may, I'd like to leave you with a word of encouragement—*beat it!* *(She mimes slamming the door.)* Boy! Some people! . . . OK, this is my last try. *(She draws another card and reads.)* "He that hath pity on the poor lendeth to the Lord." *(She puts the card back in a huff.)* This just isn't my day! Every scripture I pick doesn't seem to have any relevance whatsoever to *my* life . . . I'm just gonna have to go back to the old "Close Your Eyes and Point" technique.

(MARLENE *picks up her Bible, closes her eyes, opens the Bible, and points to a scripture. She opens her eyes, reads the scripture to herself, then shakes her head and repeats the process. As she does this, the* ANNOUNCER *speaks over the P.A.)*

ANNOUNCER: And so we come to the end of another episode of *All My Verses.* Be sure to tune in tomorrow to find out if Marlene ever does find a scripture she's willing to obey or if she will just keep skipping over verse after verse until the only one left is "Jesus wept." *(A beat)* Come to think of it . . . maybe that's what He's doing right now.

(Blackout)

Taking Stock

Character:
> HOWARD ROSE

Setting: Golden Street Stock Exchange

Props: Desk
> Chair
> Various business reports, stock exchange papers, etc.

Costumes: Modern-day wear

(Monologue opens with HOWARD seated at the desk, looking over business reports and stock papers. Then . . . as if into camera.)

This is Howard Rose with the "Taking Stock" stock report—the latest economic news to guide you on your journey from Wall Street to the Golden Streets.

Earthly treasures are continuing to decline in value. Most brokers are encouraging their clients to acquire more eternal stocks at this time. Investing in "Treasures in Heaven" stock may not let you see much gain here on earth, but their market value in the hereafter is going through the roof! Helping others, giving to the poor, visiting the widows and those in prison—you won't find these featured in the *Wall Street Journal* or *Fortune 500*, but they're *big* accounts where it matters most. And believe me, God is one broker who keeps very good books!

Again, this is Howard Rose with the "Taking Stock" report reminding you to take stock of your life daily. If you're not investing in eternal treasures, you just might want to rethink your portfolio.

(Blackout)

The Real Story

Characters:
    GARY KING: *talk show host*
    PROFESSOR RANDOLPH RUPNICK
    ADAM

Setting: The "Gary King Live Show"

Props: Table
    Three chairs
    Social Security card, numbered "1" (in ADAM's pocket)

Costumes: Shirt, pants, suspenders, and glasses for GARY KING
    Suit for PROFESSOR RUPNICK
    Leaf-wear for ADAM

(Sketch opens with GARY KING seated at the left of the table. PROFESSOR RUPNICK and ADAM are sitting across from him to the right of the table.)

GARY *(to audience):* Good evening. My guests tonight are Professor Rupnick, the world's leading authority on evolution, and . . . Adam. *(To ADAM)* Just *Adam?* No last name?

ADAM: In my day, we didn't need one.

GARY: Uh, yes, well, our topic tonight is how man came to be. His origin. His beginning. We'll start with Professor Rupnick. You, sir, believe that man evolved from the primates. Am I correct?

PROFESSOR: That is what I believe, yes.

ADAM: The primates?! You gotta be kidding! That's the most *ridiculous* thing I've ever heard.

GARY: Please, Mr., uh, Adam . . . I'll give you a chance to respond in a moment. Let the professor explain his position.

PROFESSOR: . . . Gary, after years and years of extensive scientific research, my colleagues and I have come to the conclusion that man is a direct descendent of the monkey.

ADAM: Descendent of him? I *named* him!

PROFESSOR: Do you mind? *(To GARY)* I thought this was going to be a debate between two *intellectual* minds.

GARY *(to ADAM):* You named the monkey?

ADAM: I named all the animals—elephant, giraffe *(Looks at the PROFESSOR)* . . . donkey. They were all my idea. You like "aardvark"?

GARY: I gotta admit it sure comes in handy in Scrabble. . . . So, what you're saying is you were the first man on earth?

ADAM: Now you're getting the picture. I've even got my Social Security card to prove it. *(Takes card out of pocket and shows it to him)* See. *(Pointing to the number)* . . . "One."

PROFESSOR: Gary, I'm a highly respected scientist. I don't have time for these fairy tales.

ADAM: Yeah, man evolving from monkeys . . . where did you come up with a fairy tale like that? I don't even *like* bananas.

PROFESSOR: I don't have to stay here and take this. I came here tonight to discuss *facts*.

ADAM: You want facts, Professor? I'll give you facts. *I was there!* I know firsthand what happened. One day I wasn't in existence, and the next day I was a fully grown man made in *God's* image . . . not *Bonzo's*.

GARY: So, you're a creationist?

ADAM: I prefer the term *eyewitness*.

GARY: If you were created as a grown man, then you had no childhood?

ADAM: That's right. You won't see me on the talk show circuit talking about my dysfunctional family. It was just me. I was created just as you see me now. I didn't have to go through teething, learning to walk, puberty, none of it. Same with my wife.

GARY: Your wife?

ADAM: I got lonely, so I asked the Creator for a helpmate. He gave me Eve. *(Smiling broadly)* Talk about paradise—a custom-made wife and no mother-in-law.

GARY: So then women were your idea?

ADAM *(nods):* Turned out pretty nice, don't you think?

GARY: The packaging is great, but why didn't you have them come with an instruction manual?

ADAM: I thought about it, but I figured even God was too busy to write that big of a book!

PROFESSOR: This is all mildly amusing, but can we get back to the debate now?

GARY: In a minute. *(To* ADAM*)* So where'd all this take place?

ADAM: In the Garden of Eden. We lived there until we had to move.

PROFESSOR *(sarcastically):* Property taxes too high?

ADAM: The cost of disobedience was too high. God told us we could eat the fruit of any of the trees in the Garden of Eden, except one. We disobeyed and got . . . well, I guess you could say we were evicted.

PROFESSOR: Look, I'm sure all this goes over big in Sunday School class, but I'm a highly respected scientist. I don't have time for such nonsense.

GARY: So, professor, what you're saying is that you can prove evolution beyond a shadow of a doubt?

PROFESSOR: Well, not exactly *prove* . . .

ADAM: Then, why are you teaching it as a *fact?* Isn't it still a theory?

PROFESSOR: One of these days scientists will have enough evidence to prove our theory beyond a shadow of a doubt.

ADAM: One of these days you're going to come face-to-face with the Creator, and He's going to prove His existence beyond a shadow of a doubt.

GARY: You know, professor, there *is* one thing I've always wondered about. If the theory of evolution is correct, why aren't monkeys still evolving today?

PROFESSOR: Uh . . . well, that's because . . . well, I guess, uh . . .

ADAM: The fool that said in his heart there is no God.

PROFESSOR: Are you calling me a fool, sir?

ADAM: Not me. It's in the Bible.

PROFESSOR: I simply don't believe in what I can't see.

ADAM: Can you see the millions of people who are watching us right now on their television screens?

PROFESSOR: No.

ADAM: Then they must not exist, right?

PROFESSOR: They exist. We can't see them, but we know they're there.

ADAM: God exists too. We can't see Him, but if we look all around us, we *know* He's there. There's an order to the universe, a blueprint too perfect to be chance.

GARY: So then it's all just a matter of faith?

PROFESSOR: Yeah, *blind* faith.

ADAM: Sir, it takes more faith to believe that man came to be by remarkable coincidence than it takes to believe in a remarkable God.

GARY: And on that note we'll have to close. *(To audience)* But don't forget to tune in next week when handyman Tim Allen gets some building tips from Noah. Should be interesting. Until then . . . this is Gary King. Good night.

(Blackout)

Donkey Talk

A Commercial

Characters:
> SALESMAN
> LADY 1
> MAN
> LADY 2

Setting: TV commercial

Props: Freestanding counter
> Sign on or above counter that says, *"DONKEY TALK*—Don't you want to hear what YOUR donkey has to say?"
> 20 or so videos marked *Donkey Talk*

Costumes: Bible era clothing

(Sketch opens with SALESMAN *standing behind the counter. There are a stack of eight videos on the counter. Each of them marked "Donkey Talk.")*

SALESMAN *(energetic and fast-paced):* Are you having trouble communicating with your donkey? Do you wish your beast of burden understood you better? Wouldn't it be great if he spoke your language? Well, he can! Impossible, you say? Not with my new *Donkey Talk* video series.

    We've all heard the news reports of Balaam's donkey who talked. Now yours can too. All you need is just 29.95, in shekels or credit tablet and you, too, will be conversing with your donkey in just 10 short days! *(A beat)* Some dialects slightly longer.

    Imagine finally being able to get to the bottom of those awful mood swings, to talk him through his stubbornness, and help your animal excel to his fullest potential.

    Yes, in just 10 days your donkey can master such difficult phrases as "Oh, no, not hay *again*" and "Why don't you ever carry your own stuff, man?" . . . But don't take my word for it. Let's hear from a few of our satisfied customers.

*(*LADY 1 *walks in carrying a "Donkey Talk" video and throws it down on the counter.)*

LADY 1: I bought your video over four months ago, and my donkey hasn't uttered a single word yet!

(She exits. MAN *walks in carrying a "Donkey Talk" video and throws it down on the counter.* LADY 2 *walks in behind him.)*

MAN: I want my money back and I want it back *now*. You're a fraud!

LADY 2: My donkey doesn't talk either, but if he could, the only thing he'd say to me is "Sucker!"

SALESMAN: Uh . . . perhaps you're not following the instructions *precisely.*

LADY 2: Or perhaps you're just running a nice little racket here.

MAN: Yeah, perhaps we should report you to the authorities.

SALESMAN: The . . . *authorities?*

MAN: Making people think you can teach a donkey to talk just like Balaam's donkey. That's *low,* man! Really *low!*

LADY 2: Where's the crew of *60 Minutes* when you need them?

SALESMAN: So, I take it you don't want the next video in the series—*Teaching Your Donkey the Macarena? (The two customers turn and stomp off in a huff. The* SALESMAN *turns to the audience.)* OK, so it was God, and God alone, who made Balaam's donkey speak, but a guy's gotta try to make a buck where he can . . . even if he does have to alter the facts! *(From both sides of the stage, unseen by the audience, stage hands start tossing empty "Donkey Talk" video boxes at him. As he ducks . . .)* Or maybe not.

(Blackout)

Emergency Rapture System

Character:
 ANNOUNCER (unseen)
Sound Effects: Trumpet blast

(This is an announcement that comes over the sound system only.)

ANNOUNCER: The following is a test of the Emergency Rapture System. It is only a test. *(We hear the sound of trumpets.)*

Had this been the actual Rapture, those of you who were ready would have been caught up to meet the Lord in the sky. Those of you who weren't . . . well, luckily, you've been given another chance.

Don't take it lightly, though, for according to our safety handbook, the Bible, it *is* going to happen soon and it'll happen when you least expect it. So we advise you to take all the necessary precautions and be prepared at all times.

This concludes this test of the Emergency Rapture System. We now return to our regularly scheduled programming.

Wide World of Slingshots

Characters:
  SPORTS REPORTER
  DAVID

Setting: Battlefield

Props: Slingshot
  Handheld microphone

Costumes: Modern-day wear for REPORTER
  Bible era clothing for DAVID

(Sketch opens with DAVID standing center stage, slingshot in hand. REPORTER is off to the side, holding the microphone.)

REPORTER *(softly into microphone; it should sound like a sports reporter at a golf tournament):* We're here at the front line of the battle between the Israelites and the Philistines. The giant, Goliath, has just challenged the Israelites to send in their best man, and so far the only one to step forward is David, the shepherd boy. Now David's skill with the slingshot has earned him local acclaim, but this time he may have bitten off more than he can chew. *(DAVID starts to wind up his swing.)* Let's watch as the young lad winds up his swing . . . There's a lot riding on this, folks. If David misses, Goliath is sure to rip him in two. What courage! What confidence! What . . . *(DAVID pretends to shoot; REPORTER moves his head as though following the stone through the air)* a shot! It looks good . . . yes . . . yes . . . It's a bulls-eye! Right between the . . . *(he looks up then down, as though he just watched the giant drop)* eyes. The giant is down! *(DAVID does a victory step.)* David has won the match with just one lucky shot! *(Suddenly DAVID stops, then walks toward the REPORTER.)* The champion appears to be walking this way. He must have something he wants to say to his many fans.

DAVID: Excuse me. Did I hear you say *lucky* shot?

REPORTER *(in normal voice):* Well, you gotta admit it was incredibly . . .

DAVID *(cutting in):* Luck had nothing to do with it. God was on my side.

REPORTER: Well, however you did it, it was something to see! You know the offers are going to start pouring in now—slingshot companies wanting you to be their spokesman, pro slingshot scouts trying to sign you up. I hope you've got a good agent.

DAVID: I've got the only agent I need—God. Whether He wants me to stay a shepherd boy or wants me to become king, either way, I couldn't be in better hands.

REPORTER *(as if into camera):* And there you have it, folks . . . the giant, Goliath, has been beaten and David's God adds another win to a perfect score. See you next week for another edition of *Wide World of Slingshots.*

(Blackout)

Carpenter's Corner

Characters:
> Rob Viola: *show host*
> Frank: *worker*

Setting: The "Carpenter's Corner" TV show

Props: A house built on a rock, can either be real or left to the audience's imagination
> Sand

Costumes: Modern-day work clothes
> Tool belt for Frank

(Sketch opens with Rob Viola standing next to the house built on the rock. A mound of sand is nearby.)

Rob: Today on "Carpenter's Corner" we're going to be talking about the importance of building on a good foundation. To demonstrate this, we've built two identical houses. One, as you see here, was built on a rock. The other . . . *(looks around)* well, now, that's odd. Where'd it go? It was here at rehearsal yesterday. (Frank *enters soaking wet—hair, clothes, everything.*) What happened to you?

Frank: I built a house on the sand like you said.

Rob: Yeah?

Frank: Well, this big wave came up and . . .

Rob: Don't tell me—it knocked the house over?

Frank: No. Just the patio. But while I was repairing the patio, the winds started blowing . . .

Rob: And *they* knocked the house over?

Frank: No. Blew the roof off. Then while I was repairing the roof, it started to rain . . .

Rob: And the rain knocked the house over?

Frank: No. The house finally collapsed when the flood came.

Rob: Flood?

Frank: I barely escaped with my life. Sorry, I ruined your show like this.

Rob: Ruined my show? Are you kidding? This is exactly what I wanted to happen!

FRANK: It is?

ROB: Every bit of it.

FRANK: Funny, I don't remember reading that in my contract.

ROB: Don't you see—all these calamities clearly show our viewers the importance of building on a rock!

FRANK: Couldn't we have just written a safety manual instead?

ROB: Are you kidding? A living room floating out to sea is worth a thousand words. *(As if into camera)* See, folks at home, this house that was built on a rock . . . *(indicating house on the rock)* faced the very same elements, but its builder didn't have to go through all that my buddy, Frank, here went through. And do you know why?

FRANK: *He* read his contract?

ROB: No. Because he built his house on a solid foundation!

FRANK: But you *told* me to build it on the sand.

ROB *(patting him on the back):* And you did a good job, Frank.

FRANK: But my house is floating to China right now.

ROB: And what better way to drive home my point?

FRANK: Can I go home? I don't think I'm feeling very well.

ROB: Sure, but just one last thing . . . It's important because this principle applies to life as well. *(To audience as if into camera)* Folks, remember, when you build your house be sure to . . . *(He puts the microphone at FRANK's mouth.)*

FRANK *(into microphone):* . . . build it on a rock! . . . Or read your contract!

ROB *(to audience):* This is Bob Viola of *Carpenter's Corner* saying, "Happy building!"

(They smile at the camera for a beat, then FRANK turns to ROB . . .)

FRANK: You do have Workman's Comp, don't you?

(Blackout)

Revelation Hot Line

Character:
> HOST of "Revelation Hot Line"

Setting: Desk or counter

Props: Phone
> Bible

Costume: Modern-day wear

(Sketch opens with HOST seated behind the desk. The phone and Bible are on the desk.)

Wanna know the future? Wanna be ready for what tomorrow holds? You don't have to call those other hot lines and pay outrageous fees just to know what lies ahead. We've got it all right here in this book *(holds up the Bible)*—the Holy Bible. Prophets of long ago wrote it all down under the divine inspiration of the Holy Spirit. So if you want to know the *true* future, if you want to hear from a prophet with a 100 percent accuracy record, call *Revelation Hot Line* . . . or better yet, just read the book!

. . . Got Hope?

A Commercial

Characters:
IRS OFFICE RECEPTIONIST
HERB NEWCOMB
ANNOUNCER

Setting: IRS office lobby

Props: Receptionist counter at the IRS office
Cup of coffee
Several chairs

Costumes: Modern-day wear

(Sketch opens with HERB *entering the lobby, carrying a cup of coffee. The* RECEPTIONIST *is behind the counter, chewing gum and reading a magazine. Several other taxpayers are waiting in the chairs.)*

HERB *(to himself):* OK, it's only an audit. It's not the end of the world. I've brought all my receipts, and everything's going to be . . . *(Looks toward a particular chair)* Ut-oh, where's my receipts? *(He starts looking under the chair and around the office.)* They were right here a minute ago.

RECEPTIONIST *(noticing him):* Excuse me, sir . . . are you having a problem?

HERB: As a matter of fact, yes. I just left the room a minute ago to get a cup of coffee, and now my receipts are missing.

RECEPTIONIST: What'd they look like?

HERB: They were in a grocery bag.

RECEPTIONIST: *Everybody's* receipts are in a grocery bag. Can you be more specific?

HERB: All right, it was a Piggly Wiggly bag.

RECEPTIONIST: Oh, I remember the bag.

HERB *(sighs):* Whew! What a relief.

RECEPTIONIST: I thought it was trash.

HERB: You didn't . . .

RECEPTIONIST: Sorry. We like to keep things tidy around here.

HERB *(trying to stay calm):* That's all right. I'll just dig it out of the trash.

RECEPTIONIST: Oh, we don't throw trash away. We put it through a paper shredder. (HERB *looks sick.*) . . . I've got some glue if you want to borrow it . . .

ANNOUNCER *(over P.A.):* . . . Got hope? Get Jesus.

What's Cookin'?

Characters:
    JULIA WILD
    YOUNG BOY 1
    YOUNG BOY 2

Setting: The "'What a Dish!' Cooking Show"

Props: 2 lunch bags (one with a peanut butter and jelly sandwich inside)
    Various cooking utensils, pots, etc.
    Freestanding kitchen counter

Costumes: Modern-day wear

(Sketch opens with JULIA *standing behind the counter.)*

JULIA *(in high-pitched voice):* Welcome back to the "'What a Dish!' Cooking Show." I'm Julia Wild, and for our next recipe we're going to be making fish and bread to feed 5,000 men. Now then, according to this recipe, the first thing we need is a little boy's lunch, offered freely. (YOUNG BOY 1 *walks across the stage, whistling. He's carrying a lunch sack in his hand.)* Hey, little boy . . . give me your lunch.

YOUNG BOY 1: No! It's mine! *(He presses the lunch to his chest and runs offstage.)*

JULIA: What a little mons . . . *(As if into camera)* Oh, sorry . . . I didn't realize the cameras were still rolling. (YOUNG BOY 2 *enters, carrying a lunch sack.)* . . . Hi, young man.

YOUNG BOY 2: Hey, I know you! You're the lady on that cooking show.

JULIA: That's right. In fact, you're on my show right now.

YOUNG BOY 2: I am? *(Looks toward audience as if into camera)*

JULIA: Yeah. We're live, and you kids really shouldn't be walking across my stage like this, but since you're here, would you mind if I borrowed your lunch?

YOUNG BOY 2: My lunch?

JULIA: I need it for my recipe.

YOUNG BOY 2: So, use your own lunch.

JULIA: I can't. The recipe calls for a little boy's lunch of five loaves and two fishes, and he has to (JULIA *grabs the lunch, but the* BOY *refuses to let go)* . . . give it freely.

YOUNG BOY 2: But what if I don't want to give it freely?

JULIA: C'mon. *(Tries to grab the lunch)* Millions of people are waiting for this recipe.

YOUNG BOY 2: Oh, I get it now. *I know what you're doing!*

JULIA: What am I doing?

YOUNG BOY 2: You're trying to repeat the miracle of the feeding of the 5,000.

JULIA: So what if I am? It was one of the biggest banquets in history. Now, all I need is *your lunch, so give it to me! (She wrestles it away from him.)*

YOUNG BOY 2 *(indicating lunch):* I hate to tell you this, but you're gonna need more than my little lunch to feed 5,000 men.

JULIA: I'll add a little seasoning . . . a squirt of lemon . . .

YOUNG BOY 2: You're gonna need *Jesus.* The only reason that little boy's lunch fed all those people was because *Jesus* was there.

JULIA: So, even if you give me your lunch, I'm not going to be able to feed 5,000?

YOUNG BOY 2: Nope. And besides, all I've got in here is a peanut butter and jelly sandwich.

JULIA: No fish?

YOUNG BOY 2: Sorry.

JULIA: In that case I'll just do my recipe for turning water into wine.

YOUNG BOY 2: I'm afraid you're gonna need Jesus for that miracle too.

JULIA: I am?

YOUNG BOY 2: Yep.

JULIA: So, what you're saying is Jesus is the key ingredient in all these recipes?

YOUNG BOY 2 *(nods):* And the one for true happiness too.

(Blackout)

"Lost at Sea" Update

Characters:

> ANNOUNCER
> NEWS REPORTER

Setting: The seaside

Props: Handheld microphone

Costume: Bible era wear

ANNOUNCER (*over P.A.*): We interrupt this program for this late-breaking news bulletin . . .

(*Lights come up and we see the* NEWS REPORTER *on the seashore, holding the microphone in his hand.*)

REPORTER: We have an update on the man who was lost at sea for three days. Known only as Jonah, the missing man has miraculously turned up in the city of Nineveh and is holding a revival there. Word on the street has it that he spent three days inside the belly of a big fish, then decided to quit running from God. Apparently, the people of Nineveh are listening to his message, because our sources tell us the entire city has repented. We repeat, Jonah is alive and well in the city of Nineveh. This has been a special breaking news report. We now return to our regularly scheduled programming.

(*Blackout*)

Sadducee TV

Characters:
    SADDUCEE
    WIDOW
    DIRECTOR
    PHONE STAFF (three or four people—nonspeaking roles)
    JESUS
    SEVERAL DISCIPLES

Setting: The "Sadducee TV" show

Props: Sign that says "Sadducee TV"
    Pledge thermometer
    Donation bowl, preferably metal
    Chair
    Pouch with two coins inside
    Table, chairs, and phones for phone staff
    Headset for director

Costume: Bible era clothing

(Sketch opens with SADDUCEE *sitting on the chair, speaking to the audience as if into camera. The* PHONE STAFF *are either asleep or doing their hair or filing their nails. The* DIRECTOR *is off to the side, wearing a headset.)*

SADDUCEE: Today on "Sadducee TV," we'll be wrapping up our series of messages on the 15 commandments. I know there were only 10 commandments on the original tablets that God gave to Moses, but we've added a few of our own. And don't forget, next week we'll be beginning our new study titled "If Your Brother Offend Thee, Get Even." We also want to remind you about this month's giveaway. For a donation of 100 shekels or more, we'll send you . . . (WIDOW *walks onstage, carrying a pouch. She looks a little confused.* SADDUCEE *turns to* DIRECTOR.) What's *she* doing here?

(DIRECTOR *approaches* SADDUCEE.)

DIRECTOR: I think she wants to donate some money.

SADDUCEE: Well, tell her to call our 800 number. Our operators are standing by. (*He walks over to the* PHONE STAFF *and kicks the chair of one of the operator's who's sleeping.)*

DIRECTOR: Maybe she's got so much money to give, she couldn't fit all the zeroes onto a check.

SADDUCEE: Well, what are you standing there for? Get out the donation bowl! (*As* DIRECTOR *walks over to get the donation bowl,* SADDUCEE *approaches the* WIDOW.) . . . Yes, sister, can I help you?

(The DIRECTOR walks over with the donation bowl. She reads it, smiles, and empties her pouch into it. We hear two "pings" and she walks away. SADDUCEE reaches into the bowl and counts the money.)

DIRECTOR: How much is it?

SADDUCEE: Two mites. *(Handing them to the DIRECTOR.)*

DIRECTOR: A farthing? We don't even have that mark on our money meter.

SADDUCEE: I can't believe I wasted all that air time for just *two measly mites!*

DIRECTOR: Maybe she doesn't know we take credit cards. Should I go stop her?

SADDUCEE: Good idea. *(JESUS and his DISCIPLES enter.)* Wait. More visitors.

DIRECTOR: Isn't that Jesus?

SADDUCEE: Oh, no, not *Him* again.

DIRECTOR: What do you think He wants?

JESUS *(to his DISCIPLES as they walk across the stage):* Did you see the offering that widow gave? She gave more than anyone else. She gave all she had. *(JESUS and his DISCIPLES exit.)*

DIRECTOR: Did you hear that? He was impressed with an offering of just *two mites?*

SADDUCEE: He just doesn't get it, does He? Two mites won't buy us anything. It won't buy us new robes, it won't pay our dinner at the finest hotel in town, it won't do us any good at all. That man, or "Son of God" as He prefers to call himself, just doesn't understand the principle of giving.

DIRECTOR *(looking at the two mites in his hand, then thoughtfully):* Maybe we're the ones who don't understand.

(Blackout)

Evening at the Desert Improv

Characters:
>ANNOUNCER
>HAMIR

Setting: The Desert Improv should look like a comedy club in Bible times
Props: Microphone on stand
>Cell phone

Costumes: Bible era clothing
Sound Effects:
>Rim Shot
>Thunder
>Rain

(Sketch opens with ANNOUNCER *standing at the microphone.)*

ANNOUNCER: Welcome back to the Desert Improv, the world's *very first* comedy club. Are you having a good time so far? *(Motions for audience to applaud)* Well, there's more to come, so just sit back and get ready to laugh your sandals off with our next guest. You've seen him on B.C. Comics Live! Nomads of Laughter, and The Comedy Tent. Let's give it up now for tonight's headliner . . . Hamir! *(He leads the audience in applause as* HAMIR *energetically enters and approaches the microphone.* ANNOUNCER *exits.)*

HAMIR: Thank you, thank you. *(While motioning for them to continue . . .)* No, no, stop. You're too kind . . . Sorry I'm a little late, but man oh man, you wouldn't believe the trouble I had gettin' here tonight. There's this guy who lives on my block—goes by the name of Noah . . . We just call him "The Old Man and No Sea," because he's building this ark, right there in his front yard. The thing's 50 cubits wide and 30 cubits high . . . I guess that's one way to get out of mowing the grass. *(SFX: rim shot.)* Anyway, I think everyone in town was driving by his house. Talk about a traffic jam! And get this . . . he says the reason he's doing it is that God told him a flood's coming. A flood . . . in the middle of a desert! . . . If you ask me, ol' Noah's not getting enough fresh air between those coats of varnish . . . you know what I mean? *(SFX: rim shot.)*

>Yeah, he says it's going to rain 40 days and 40 nights. Either he's wacko or he owns stock in an umbrella company. *(SFX: clap of thunder.)* . . . Hey, don't panic, folks. That's nothing. My wife snores louder than that. *(SFX: another clap of thunder, then the sound of rain. As if to audience.)* Hey, c'mon . . . where're you going? Don't tell me I'm getting upstaged by a little cloudburst. *(SFX: rain grows even louder.)* . . . OK, a *big* cloudburst! But stick around. I'm just getting to my "A" material. Besides, you can't believe Noah. The guy's 600 years old. He probably hears a lot of voices, not just God's. *(SFX: big clap of thunder.)* . . . *Of course, God's voice is probably the*

loudest. . . . Oh, all right, be that way. I don't need an audience. I'll just . . . (Thinks for a moment) Ummm . . . maybe Noah could use some entertainment on that cruise ship of his. I'll call my agent. *(He takes cell phone out of pocket and dials.)* Yo, Bernie . . . Hamir here. Howza 'bout getting me a gig on Noah's cruise ship? *(Exiting)* Really? . . . Well, it won't be the first time I've performed for a bunch of animals. So can you book it? It could be a great gig. *(SFX: thunder clap. Looks up.)* . . . The guy's obviously got connections in high places . . . What do you mean, the door's closed? Pull some strings . . . I don't know. That's what I pay *you* for. *(SFX: one last loud clap of thunder.)* . . . Look, all I know is if you don't do something quick *(SFX: loud rain.)*, I'm gonna be all washed up in this business! *(Closes cell phone, puts it back in his pocket and exits, trying to duck the rain)*

(Blackout)

. . . Got Peace?

A Commercial

Character:
MITCH HARRIS
Setting: The freeway in rush hour traffic
Props: Steering wheel
      Chair
Costume: Modern-day wear
Sound Effects: Car horn

(Monologue opens with MITCH *sitting on the chair center stage. He's holding the steering wheel in front of him.)*

     C'mon! Get out of my way! *(SFX: horn. Calls out his window.)* If you're going to go that slow, drive a tractor! . . . Yeah, well the same to you, buddy! . . . I don't believe this traffic! I've got a lunch meeting in 15 minutes, a report due by three o'clock, and a presentation to give before the end of the day. *(SFX: honks horn.)* C'mon, move it! *(SFX: horn.)* Move it! Move it! Move it! *(Turns to his side, then gulps)* . . . Uh, no, no . . . I didn't mean *you*, officer. *(Suddenly,* MITCH *looks a little sick.)*

ANNOUNCER *(over P.A.):* . . . Got peace? . . . Get Jesus.

Sowin' Seeds

Characters:
MARTHA STUBERT
DARYL

Setting: The "Martha Stubert Gardening Show"—garden setting

Props: Sign that says "Martha Stubert Gardening Show"
Various garden signs, including ones marked "Carrots" and "Cucumbers"
Various vegetables, including a potato and tomatoes
Dirt

Costume: Gardening wear, modern-day

(Sketch opens with MARTHA *working in her garden. The garden signs are posted in alphabetical order.)*

MARTHA *(to audience, as if into camera):* Hello, and welcome to the "Martha Stubert Gardening Show." Thank you for joining me. You'll recall earlier in the season we planted vegetables in our little garden here. It's now time to harvest. Let's start with our carrots, shall we? *(Moves to the "Carrots" sign)* Oh, my . . . don't they look lovely? . . . We'll just pull one of the plants up like this and . . . *(She pulls at the plant, but a potato comes up instead.)* Wait a minute. This isn't a carrot. It's a *potato! (Looks at sign again)* The sign *says* "Carrots," but this is definitely a *potato* . . . Oh well, just because it has eyes doesn't mean it can read. We'll move on to another plant. *(She moves to the sign that says "Cucumbers.")* Why don't we see what our cucumbers are doing? *(She looks for a cucumber on that plant, but finds a tomato instead. She picks it and holds it up.)* Apparently, they're impersonating tomatoes! *(Calling offstage)* . . . All right, who switched my signs? . . . Does someone need a little Martha Stubert etiquette lesson to keep their grubby little mitts off other people's property? . . . Excuse me a minute, folks. *(Calling offstage)* Daryl!

*(*DARYL *enters, timidly.)*

DARYL: Yes, Ms. Stubert . . . ?

MARTHA: Would you mind telling me what's going on here?

DARYL: Is something wrong?

MARTHA: *Somebody* mixed up all my garden signs. That *somebody* wouldn't happen to be *you*, would it?

DARYL: I thought I'd alphabetize them for you.

MARTHA: Alphabetize them?

DARYL: Yeah. I figured it'd make things easier on you.

MARTHA: Easier? Do you realize what you've done? How am I supposed to know *what* I've planted, and *where* I've planted it, if you've mixed up all the signs?

DARYL: That's easy. You just do what you're doing now. Wait and see what comes up.

MARTHA: *Wait and see what comes up?* That's not how you run a gardening show!

DARYL: You want me to put the signs back where you had them?

MARTHA: Yes, and please don't ever do that again!

DARYL: I promise. But you have to admit it was a good lesson in living life.

MARTHA: How do you figure that?

DARYL: We're all gonna reap what we sow no matter how many times someone changes the signs.

MARTHA *(thinks about that for a beat):* You know, Daryl, sometimes your brilliance amazes me!

(Blackout)

Eternity Awards Show

HOST

Setting: The "Eternity Awards Show" taking place at the Pearly Gates Pavilion
Props: Handheld microphone
Costume: White robe

Coming to you live from the Pearly Gates Pavilion, it's the event of a lifetime, the awards show of all awards shows, the one that's had the entire world talking from generation to generation—it's the "Eternity Awards Show"!

I tell you, folks, anybody who's anybody has turned up today. Famous faces you've heard so much about: Peter, Matthew, Martin Luther, Billy Sunday, the list goes on and on—legends of our faith. If you don't have a ticket to *this* ceremony, you are definitely not in the "in" crowd!

Yes, this is the one, the big event, the day folks have been anticipating for thousands and thousands of years, and it's guaranteed to be full of surprises. Who will be the big winners? Will it be those saints who were always in the spotlight or those faithful servants we never heard about.

The records have been kept sealed through the centuries and are known only to the accounting firm of Father, Son, and Holy Ghost.

The ceremony will be beginning any moment now, and from what I hear, the celebration is sure to last throughout eternity! Talk about a party!

We'll have full coverage of all the presentations right after this life . . . so stay tuned. It'll be well worth the wait!

(Blackout)

Solomon's Court TV

Characters:
    DOUG STUBEN
    MOTHER 1
    MOTHER 2
    BABY (doll may be used)
Setting: Just outside King Solomon's Court
Props: Handheld microphone
Costumes: Suit for DOUG STUBEN

(Sketch opens with DOUG standing just outside King Solomon's court.)

DOUG *(into handheld microphone):* Well, there you have it, folks. Solomon has given us his ruling in the case of Mother vs. Mother. Both women were claiming to have given birth to the same baby. Since there's no way of testing blood type, DNA, or fingerprints, and the "Geraldo Show" doesn't air here, we had a real dilemma on our hands. But King Solomon, in his profound wisdom, came up with the perfect solution. He ordered the baby be divided between the two women . . . literally. I don't think he really would have done it, but he knew his verdict would reveal the *true* mother. And it did. We're going to be speaking with both the plaintiff and the defendant in this case as soon as they . . . (MOTHER 1 *and* MOTHER 2 *enter.* MOTHER 2 *is carrying the* BABY.) Ah . . . here they come now . . . Ladies, what did you think of the outcome of this case?

MOTHER 1: I was *tricked!*

DOUG: Tricked?

MOTHER 1: Yes. King Solomon stooped to trickery and scare tactics . . . I thought he was a king, not an attorney.

DOUG: So you didn't think it was a brilliant piece of legal maneuvering?

MOTHER 1: Of course it was brilliant. But it didn't get me that baby!

DOUG: But the baby wasn't yours.

MOTHER 1: Details. Besides, I would have treated him just like my own son. I would have hired someone to take him to his Little League games, given him his own TV so he'd stay out of my hair, and on those weekends when I'd leave him home alone while I partied, I'd let him order all the pizza he wanted.

DOUG *(sarcastically):* You would have been willing to do all that?

MOTHER 1: In a heartbeat.

MOTHER 2: Well, sorry, but the judge already gave his ruling. I have my baby back, and all's right with the world.

MOTHER 1: Well, would you at least let me visit him on weekends?

MOTHER 2: Sure.

MOTHER 1: And will you invite me to his birthday parties?

MOTHER 2: I'd be happy to.

MOTHER 1 *(smiles warmly):* Thanks . . . Would you mind letting me hold him just one last time before I leave?

MOTHER 2: Of course. *(She hands her the* BABY.*)* You can even change him if you want.

MOTHER 1: *Change him? (She hands him back.) . . . What do I look like? His mother? (Exits)*

DOUG: Well, there you have it, folks. Truth always triumphs in the end. So, the next time you have a problem, don't take the law into your own hands, you take 'em to the king. King Solomon's Court, serving all your legal needs.

(Blackout)

On the Road Again

Character:

    DAVIS HOLMES: *news traffic reporter*

Setting: News helicopter

Props: Headset

Costume: Modern-day wear

(Monologue opens with DAVIS *in the news helicopter.)*

This is Davis Holmes in NewsCopter 6 with your daily traffic report. Not much has changed on Narrow Road. It's still the best commute there is. I don't know why more people don't take this route. The directions are clearly posted so you won't get lost. There's never a detour . . . unless you choose to take one. And you won't see any bumper battles over who's going to be in the lead. In fact, on this road, it's considered an honor to be in last place.

Wish I could say the same about Wide Highway. We're talkin' pure gridlock here. Bumper to bumper to bumper all the way. And cars are *still* trying to get on. I don't get it. There are hundreds of potholes to trip you up, misleading street signs, and the road rage here is epidemic. Is this *anyone's* idea of fun?

I'd recommend bypassing all this misery by taking the Narrow Road exit the first chance you get. Don't be fooled into thinking the road more traveled is the better way to go. These people are just following the crowd and getting nowhere fast. Narrow Road is the route that's going to get you where you want to go.

So, take it from me, Davis Holmes, your NewsCopter 6 traffic reporter. Take Narrow Road while you still can. I witness people honking and tailgating and cutting each other off on Wide Highway every day. If they could only see what I see, where it's leading—to a dead end.

(Blackout)

. . . Got Love?

A Commercial

Characters:
> BARTENDER
> JOE

Setting: Nightclub
> (Note to the director: You can give the appearance of a bar without using real bottles, etc.)

Props: Several glasses
> Freestanding counter
> Barstool

Costumes: Modern-day wear

(Sketch opens with BARTENDER *standing behind counter.* JOE *is seated on a barstool in front of him.)*

JOE: Give me another.

BARTENDER: This isn't what you want.

JOE: How do you know what I want?

BARTENDER: 'Cause I've seen it in the eyes of a hundred guys just like you.

JOE: Well, now it's 101. Look, just give me another and make it strong. I've got a lot of memories that are just begging to be washed away.

BARTENDER: I can do that, but tomorrow you're going to wake up just as lonely as you are today.

JOE: What difference does it make to you?

BARTENDER: None. But there might be someone out there who cares what you do with your life.

JOE: If there is, I'd sure like to meet 'im.

*(*BARTENDER *hands* JOE *another drink. As* JOE *downs it, then buries his head in his hands.)*

ANNOUNCER *(over P.A.):* . . . Got love? . . . Get Jesus.

(Blackout)

This Was Your Life

Characters:
>HOST
>MIKE STAPLETON
>HAROLD GREENLEY
>MARY CRAWFORD
>ROXANNE O'CONNOR
>BRAD JONES

Setting: The "This Was Your Life" set

Props: Handheld microphone

Costumes: White robes for HOST, MIKE, MARY, and HAROLD
>Modern-day outfits for ROXANNE and BRAD

(Sketch opens with our HOST and MIKE standing center stage. HOST is holding microphone.)

HOST: Welcome to another edition of "This Was Your Life." Tonight, we're going to be paying tribute to a quiet man, a humble man, a man few people knew by name, but everyone knew his smile. Mike Stapleton . . . *this was your life* . . . (HOST *leads the audience in applause as* MIKE *enters.)* Are you ready, Mike?

MIKE: As ready as I'll ever be.

HOST: Then let's start meeting some people from your past.

HAROLD *(over P.A.)*: I'm Harold Greenley, one of your coworkers. *(Enters and continues talking)* I picked up the tract you left in the lunchroom one day. You probably thought it just ended up in the trash, but it didn't. I waited until everyone left, then walked over and picked it up . . . See, I was going through this really tough time in my life, and the words in that tract—about how much God loves me—well, they got me thinking. I said the prayer that was printed on the back and turned my life over to the Lord. That next week I got transferred to another office and never got the chance to thank you . . . until now.

MIKE: I had no idea . . .

*(*HAROLD *hugs* MIKE, *then stands over to the side.)*

HOST: There's more . . .

MARY *(over P.A.)*: My name's Mary Crawford. I was the waitress at the coffee shop where you ate every Thursday morning. *(She enters and continues talking.)* Week after week you'd bow your head and say grace. Not enough people do that anymore, so a waitress notices that sort of thing. You always had something encouraging to say to me too. I never thanked you properly, but you really had an affect on my life. I didn't get a lot of encouragement. Maybe that's why yours meant so much. (MARY *walks over and hugs* MIKE.) Thanks.

MIKE: I don't even remember what I said.

MARY: I never forgot it.

ROXANNE (*over P.A.*): I was the lady at the grocery store last week. I stood in line behind you. (*Enters and continues talking*) Roxanne O'Connor's my name, but you don't know me. I watched the clerk overchange you. Since you were wearing that Christian T-shirt, I knew what I was in for next. You were going to hold up the entire line while you gave the money back. I was in a hurry and let you know it by my body language. As it turned out, I didn't need to because you didn't say a word. You took the extra money and walked out of the store. Maybe you were in a hurry, too, that day . . . and I know I shouldn't have let that one incident affect me so. But I did. After that, whenever I was confronted with a similar situation, I thought of what you did and I kept the money too. Thanks for easing my conscience.

MIKE: No, no. You were right. I never should have . . . wait, where's your robe?

ROXANNE: They won't let me stay here.

MIKE: You mean . . . ? (*She walks offstage. To* HOST . . .) Wait. I need to apologize.

HOST: No time for that. Should've done it sooner. Gotta move on.

BRAD (*over P.A.*): I'm Brad Jones. I worked at the video rental store by your house. (*Enters and continues talking*) I think I even saw you in church a few times when I visited there. You got up onstage and made some announcements. Even shook my hand afterward, but I don't think you knew who I was. (*A beat*) I always wondered why you rented the kind of movies you did—the ones you had to get from behind the counter. Oh, I know it's a free country and all, and I should have kept my eyes on the Lord and not man, but I was disappointed and never went back to your church. I'm not blaming you for the way *my* life turned out. We all make our own choices. But I was searching for a church or someone who walked what they talked . . . I quit looking after that.

MIKE: I had no idea so many people were watching my life.

HOST: Well, Mike, you know what they say . . . you win some and you lose some. But don't let it get you down. The effects of your actions, good or bad, only last . . . an eternity. (*To audience, as if into camera*) Well, that's all we have time for today, but join us again next week when we just might look you in the eye and say, *This Was Your Life . . . what did you do with it?*

(*Blackout*)

How Many of These Lillenas Collections from the Martha Bolton Catalog Have You Seen?

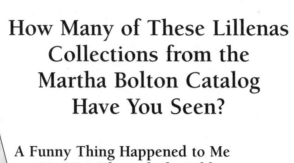

A Funny Thing Happened to Me on My Way Through the Bible

The first, and still all-time best-seller that makes 16 Bible stories come alive with great humor. (MP-628)

A View from the Pew

A popular collection of 12 sketch scripts and monologues about church life—from the potluck to the bored meeting. (MP-633)

Journey to the Center of the Stage

There's nothing quite like these 20 monologues for men and women that cover such necessary issues as visiting the sick, a choir ministry, and spending time with your children. (MP-658)

Home, Home on the Stage

A master of ceremonies guide with material that covers appeals, Valentine's Day programs, honoring parents, stewardship, comedy intros, situation savers, and roasts. (MP-667)

The "How'd I Get to Be in Charge of the Program" Help Book

An almanac of programming resources for the local church—January through December. (MP-648)

Tangled in the Tinsel

These 19 humorous scripts look at the many moods of Christmas through the medium of sketches and monologues. Ideal for banquets and other social events. (MC-268)